The Cat in the Hat's Learning Library

The editors would like to thank
BARBARA KIEFER, Ph.D.,
Charlotte S. Huck Professor of Children's Literature,
The Ohio State University, and
JIM BREHENY,
Director, Bronx Zoo,
for their assistance in the preparation of this book.

Visit us on the Web!
Seussville.com
randomhousekids.com

Educators and librarians, for a variety of teaching tools, visit us at
RHTeachersLibrarians.com

Library of Congress Cataloging-in-Publication Data
Worth, Bonnie.
Safari, so good! : all about African wildlife / by Bonnie Worth ; illustrated by Aristides Ruiz and
Joe Mathieu. — 1st ed.
   p. cm. — (The cat in the hat's learning library)
ISBN 978-0-375-86681-4 (trade) — ISBN 978-0-375-96681-1 (lib. bdg.)
1. Animals—Africa—Juvenile literature. 2. Safaris—Africa—Juvenile literature.
I. Ruiz, Aristides, ill. II. Mathieu, Joseph, ill. III. Title.
QL336.W67 2011   591.96—dc22   2010025339

Printed in the United States of America   20 19 18 17 16 15 14 13 12 11 10

Safari, So Good!

by Bonnie Worth

illustrated by Aristides Ruiz and Joe Mathieu

The Cat in the Hat's Learning Library®

Random House 🏠 New York

I'm the Cat in the Hat.
Pack your bag. Come with me.
We're going to Africa
on safari!

Pack your sunglasses
and your sun hat.
Remember your camera.
Do not forget that!

You've got front-row seats
in my Animal Viewer,
the truck we will take
on our African tour!

In the African Game Park,
we will be getting
the chance to see wildlife
in a natural setting.

AFRICAN GAME PARK

8

But here is a fact
I will tell you today.
Animals are predators
or else they are prey.

Predators hunt weaker
animals to munch.
Prey tries hard NOT
to be a predator's lunch.

Off to the river
we will go first.
Here animals come
to quench their thirst.

Look at those warthogs
trip-trot over there.
Mom, dad, and piglets,
with tails in the air.

African buffalo
graze where it's wet.
Their horns have the look
of a sturdy helmet.

Grass—ninety pounds!—
a hippo eats nightly.
Are the babies called calves?
Yes, you have guessed rightly!

A hippo's skin can
burn in the sun's rays.
Mud and water protect her,
so that's where she stays.

Let's move on to the lions,
with their tawny hides!
They live all together
in groups known as prides.

A cub has brown spots
from his tail to his ear.
At three months of age,
all those spots disappear.

Lions like sleeping—
for most of the day!
Their roars rattle windows
from miles away.

I'll name you a cat
that one rarely sees.
That cat is the leopard,
who hangs out in trees.

A leopard's black spots
come in very neat sets
of circular patterns
that are called rosettes.

She stalks, runs, and leaps
to hunt down her prey.
She hunts in the night
and she sleeps in the day.

The cheetah is covered
with sleek, spotted fur.
The cheetah can't roar.
But, oh, can she purr!

With long and strong legs,
the cheetah has power
to run up to seventy
miles an hour!

Cheetahs run fast,
and here is the scoop:
cubs sometimes play soccer
with elephant poop!

16

Speaking of elephants,
here is the word:
fifty or so
can be in one herd.

Male elephants can grow
to eleven feet high
and weigh over ten tons.
Hello there, big guy!

Calves walk from day one
and have some body hair,
which soon all rubs off
due to life's wear and tear.

The whole herd will circle
and sound the alarm
and crowd round the young ones
to keep them from harm.

The elephant's tusks
are tools, as you see,
for scraping up roots
or the bark off a tree.

They also will use
their tusks in a fight.
And they tend to favor
the left or the right.

And just as one hand
of yours is the stronger,
one of an elephant's
tusks can be longer.

The trunk is the elephant's
very long nose,
which can lift heavy things,
or spray like a hose,

or pick up one single
blade of green grass,

or *blat* like a tuba
that's made out of brass.

Two kinds of rhinos?
Oh, you are so right!
One is called black.
The other's called white.

But both rhinos are gray
in Dick's camera's sight,
so how do we tell
the black from the white?

A white rhino's lips
are wide like a bow.
He nibbles at grass,
his head hanging low.

A black rhino's lips
are agile. With these
he reaches out to crop
low leaves from the trees.

Is that oxpecker bird
hitching a ride?
No, she's eating the ticks
on the white rhino's hide.

The zebra belongs
to the horse family.
Those stripes tend to make
her quite tricky to see.

They all look alike,
but please bear this in mind.
Each zebra has stripes
that are one-of-a-kind.

Zebras rarely lie down
and sleep on the ground.
They sleep standing up.
Predators might be around!

And here is a question
to stump you, all right.
Are they white with black stripes
or else black striped with white?

At birth, giraffes drop
six feet to the ground!
In minutes, they're standing
and looking around.

All giraffes forage,
it is plain to see.
Here's one with her head in
an acacia tree.

Her eighteen-inch tongue
and her tough, spongy lips
help her to eat
the leaves' sharp, thorny tips.

Giraffes have big eyes
with long lashes that bat
at the dust and the grit
and the bugs and all that.

With strong legs and hooves
and a good bit of trying,
they can often outrun
a lioness or lion.

Baboons band together
in big, roving groups.
They hunt, eat, and sleep
in these bands we call troops.

Baboons have sharp teeth,
and they walk on all fours.
They eat plants and meat,
so they are omnivores!

Baboons are big pickers
of each other's fur.
They pick till they find
every tick, flea, and burr.

Grooming is the word that
we use when we mean
to describe how baboons
pick to keep themselves clean.

When danger is looming, baboons shout, *Wahoo!* This means "Go away! We are not kidding you!"

Safari, so good!
Let's find a campsite,
where we'll pitch our tent
and stay for the night.

The dog over there
is the side-striped jackal.
He welcomes his mate
with a loud, howling cackle.

VULTURE

OWL

BUSH RABBIT

GALAGO

The galago's eyes,
when they catch the light,
glow green like a cat's
in the dark of the night.

The spotted hyena
goes looking to eat
the dead or the dying—
a scavenger's treat.

Scavengers are those
who live for a taste
of leftovers that might
otherwise go to waste.

In the wee morning hours,
herds of antelope roam.
Over twenty kinds call
Mother Africa home.

We have just enough time
to look at a few.
So I'll pick out some different
kinds to show you.

Eland is the largest.
It measures six feet.
The royal antelope?
Ten inches—petite!

And don't miss the sight,
whatever you do,
of the twirly-horned,
handsome greater kudu.

Impalas are smaller.
Here's how to ID them.
Stripes on their rear ends
form a bold letter M.

A head like an ox
and a mane like a horse?
A beard like a goat?
A wildebeest, of course!

Let's find just one more
antelope if we're able:
the bashful, soft-coated,
sickle-horned sable!

All of these antelope
can run fast, and so
the fast will survive.
Not as often, the slow.

Our safari is ending, but
for goodness' sakes,
let's stop for one look at
my two favorite snakes.

This mighty rock python
squeezes its prey.
Snakes called constrictors
behave in this way.

The carpet viper's a small snake
that everyone heeds.
Its fangs inject poison.
It lurks in the weeds.

Safari, so good!
Home again, like a shot.
Just look at the great
photographs that we got!

Which ones are your favorites?
Which turned out the best?
Some turned out all fuzzy,
but we'll save the rest.

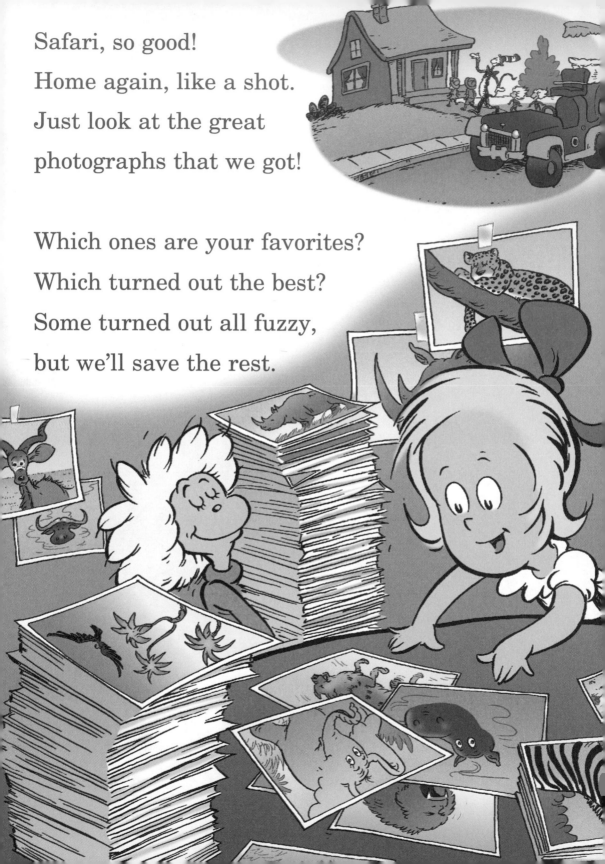

My number one favorite?

Oh, take a wild guess!

If you said the lions . . .

. . . I'd have to say YES!

GLOSSARY

Constrictor: Any snake that tightly wraps itself around its prey to strangle it.

Forage: To search for food.

ID: Another way to say the word *identify*, which means to recognize.

Inject: To force or drive a liquid into something.

Omnivore: An animal that eats everything available, both meat and plants.

Petite: Small and slender.

Predator: An animal that lives by hunting and eating others.

Prey: An animal that is hunted for food.

Quench: To satisfy or put an end to.

Sickle: A tool used for cutting that has a curved metal blade.

Sturdy: Built of strong stuff.

FOR FURTHER READING

Elephants of Africa by Gail Gibbons (Holiday House). All about elephants—their bodies, behavior, and survival strategies. For ages 5–8.

Face to Face with Lions by Beverly and Dereck Joubert (National Geographic Children's Books, *Face to Face*). Fantastic photos bring you up close to lions. For ages 6–9.

Giraffes by Jill Anderson (NorthWord Books for Young Readers, *Wild Ones*). Close-up photos follow a day in the life of a giraffe. For ages 4–8.

Here Is the African Savanna by Madeleine Dunphy (Hyperion Books for Children, *Web of Life*). Shows the interaction of plants and animals on the African savanna. For ages 4–8.

We All Went on Safari by Laurie Krebs, illustrated by Julia Cairns (Barefoot Books). A group of people travel across Tanzania—and learn to count to ten in Swahili! For ages 4–8.

INDEX